How to win th
with A

Thomas Spiteri

ISBN- 9798372839793
ISBN-10: 1477123456

Cover design by: Art Painter
Library of Congress Control Number: 2018675309
Printed in the United States of America

Chapters

Introduction: The Role of Artificial Intelligence in
Lottery Prediction

1. Understanding the Probabilities: A Statistical
   Approach to Lottery Prediction
2. Analyzing Historical Data: Using Machine
   Learning to Identify Patterns and Trends
3. Developing a Winning Strategy: Tips and
   Tricks for Improving Your Chances of
   Winning
4. Advanced Techniques: Leveraging Quantum
   Computing and Other Advanced
   Technologies to Boost Your Odds
5. Case Studies: Real-World Examples of AI-
   Powered Lottery Winners
6. Ethical Considerations: The Debate Over
   Using AI to Play the Lottery
7. Future of AI in Lottery Prediction: Exploring
   the Potential and Limitations of AI in Lottery
   Prediction
8. Conclusion: The Impact of AI on Lottery
   Prediction and the Future of Gambling
9. Bonus Chapter: Alternative Methods for
   Increasing Your Chances of Winning the
   Lottery, Including Traditional Strategies and
   Psychological Techniques

Introduction
The Role of Artificial Intelligence in Lottery Prediction

Gone are the days when lottery players were forced to rely on sheer luck and gut instinct when choosing their numbers. Today, with the rise of artificial intelligence (AI), it is possible to use advanced algorithms and data analysis to predict the most likely winning numbers for a given lottery draw. In this book, we will explore the role of AI in lottery prediction and provide you with practical tips and strategies for using AI to improve your chances of winning.

We will begin by looking at the basics of probability and how it can be used to understand the odds of winning the lottery. We will then delve into the use of machine learning and data analysis to identify patterns and trends in historical data, and how this information can be used to make informed predictions. We will also explore some of the advanced techniques and technologies that are being used by lottery players, including quantum computing and other cutting-edge approaches.

Throughout the book, we will be drawing on real-world examples and case studies to illustrate the potential of AI in lottery prediction, and to provide you with practical guidance on how you can use these techniques to improve your chances of winning. We will also consider some of the ethical considerations surrounding the use of AI in lottery prediction and explore the potential and limitations of this technology.

So, if you are ready to take your lottery game to the next level and increase your chances of winning, this book is for you. Whether you are a seasoned lottery player or a newcomer to the game, we hope that you will find valuable insights and useful tips in these pages.

Chapter 1
Understanding the Probabilities: A Statistical Approach to Lottery Prediction

Before we delve into the specific techniques and technologies that can be used to predict lottery numbers, it is important to have a basic understanding of the probabilities involved. Understanding the odds of winning the lottery can help you make more informed decisions about which numbers to choose and how to increase your chances of winning.

There are several key factors that determine the probability of winning the lottery, including the number of possible combinations of numbers, the number of balls drawn in the lottery, and the size of the pool of numbers from which the balls are drawn. For example, in a lottery with 49 balls and 6 numbers drawn, the probability of matching all 6 numbers is 1 in 13,983,816. This means that, on average, it would take 13,983,816 attempts to win the lottery by matching all 6 numbers.

Of course, the probability of winning the lottery also depends on the specific numbers that you choose. Some numbers are drawn more frequently than others, and by analyzing historical data, it is possible to identify patterns and trends that can help you choose numbers with a higher probability of being drawn. We will discuss this in more detail in the next chapter.

In the meantime, it is important to keep in mind that the probability of winning the lottery is extremely low, regardless of the specific numbers that you choose. However, by understanding the probabilities and using statistical analysis to inform your choices, you can increase your chances of winning and potentially improve your odds of success.

Chapter 2
Using Machine Learning and Data Analysis to
Identify Patterns and Trends

One of the key ways that artificial intelligence (AI) can be used to predict lottery numbers is through the use of machine learning and data analysis. By analyzing large datasets of historical lottery results, it is possible to identify patterns and trends that may not be immediately obvious to the human eye.

Using machine learning algorithms, it is possible to identify relationships between different variables and predict future outcomes with a high degree of accuracy. For example, if certain numbers are consistently drawn more frequently than others, a machine learning algorithm could be used to identify this trend and predict that these numbers are more likely to be drawn in the future.

In addition to identifying patterns and trends, data analysis can also be used to identify unusual or unexpected results, which may indicate an outlier or a deviation from the norm. By analyzing these deviations, it is possible to gain insights into the underlying causes and identify potential trends that may not be immediately apparent.

While machine learning and data analysis are powerful tools for predicting lottery numbers, it is important to remember that they are only as accurate as the data that they are based on. Therefore, it is essential to use high-quality data sources and ensure that the data is accurate and up-to-date. We will discuss this in more detail in the next chapter.

Chapter 3
Developing a Winning Strategy: Tips and Tricks for Improving Your Chances of Winning

In this chapter, we will discuss various strategies and techniques that can improve your chances of winning the lottery using AI. We will start by exploring the importance of having a clear and defined strategy, including setting goals and establishing a budget. Next, we will discuss the benefits of diversifying your portfolio, including playing multiple lotteries and using different types of AI models. We will also cover the importance of analyzing and understanding past results and how to use this information to inform your predictions. Finally, we will discuss the benefits of collaborating with others, including joining lottery pools and seeking the advice of experts. By the end of this chapter, you will have a range of strategies and tips to improve your chances of winning the lottery using AI.

1. One tip for improving your chances of winning the lottery is to diversify your ticket selections. Instead of choosing the same numbers every time or using quick pick to randomly select numbers, consider using a combination of different numbers that you have chosen based on statistical analysis or personal significance. This can increase the chances that at least some of your numbers will be drawn.

2. Another tip is to consider the trade-off between the number of tickets you play and your likelihood of winning. While it may seem tempting to buy multiple tickets in the hopes of increasing your chances, the reality is that each additional ticket you buy only slightly increases your chances of winning. Instead, consider carefully analyzing the odds and choosing your ticket selections based on probability rather than sheer quantity.

3. In addition, consider joining a syndicate or pooling your resources with a group of friends or co-workers. This can allow you to buy a larger number of tickets, thereby increasing your chances of winning, without breaking the bank. Just be sure to carefully consider the terms of the agreement and the allocation of winnings among the group.

4. Finally, consider using AI and machine learning techniques to analyze historical data and identify patterns and trends that may increase your chances of selecting winning numbers. While there are no guarantees in the lottery, using these tools can help you make more informed decisions and potentially improve your chances of winning.

Chapter 4
Advanced Techniques: Leveraging Quantum Computing and Other Advanced Technologies to Boost Your Odds

In this chapter, we will delve into advanced techniques for boosting your odds of winning the lottery. We will start by exploring the potential of quantum computing and how it can be applied to lottery prediction. Quantum computers have the ability to perform certain calculations much faster than classical computers, which could potentially allow for more accurate predictions. However, the use of quantum computers for lottery prediction is still in its early stages and there are many challenges that need to be overcome.

Next, we will discuss other advanced technologies that could potentially be used to improve lottery prediction, such as artificial neural networks and deep learning. These techniques have been shown to be effective in a variety of applications, and there is potential for them to be applied to lottery prediction as well.

We will also cover the potential limitations and ethical considerations of using advanced technologies for lottery prediction. It is important to carefully consider the potential consequences of using these technologies and to ensure that they are used ethically and responsibly.

Finally, we will explore case studies of successful applications of advanced technologies in lottery prediction, as well as challenges and lessons learned. By the end of this chapter, you will have a better understanding of the potential and limitations of advanced technologies in lottery prediction and how they can be used to improve your odds of winning.

1. Advanced techniques in lottery prediction using artificial intelligence and machine learning include leveraging quantum computing and other advanced technologies to boost your odds of winning. Quantum computing has the potential to significantly improve the performance of machine learning algorithms by allowing for faster and more accurate calculations. Other advanced technologies that may be used include natural language processing, computer vision, and deep learning. By incorporating these techniques into your lottery prediction strategy, you may be able to improve your chances of winning by identifying patterns and trends that may not be apparent using more traditional methods.

One ethical consideration is the fairness of using advanced technologies to give some players an advantage over others. Some may argue that it is not fair for a select few to have access to these technologies and potentially increase their chances of winning significantly, while others do not have the same resources.

There are also legal considerations to consider, as the use of certain advanced technologies may be restricted or banned in certain jurisdictions. It is important to familiarize yourself with the laws and regulations in your area to ensure that you are not breaking any rules by using these techniques.

Additionally, there are potential risks to consider when using advanced technologies, such as the possibility of data breaches or security vulnerabilities. It is important to take necessary precautions to protect your data and secure your systems to minimize these risks.

Overall, the potential benefits of using advanced techniques to boost your odds of winning the lottery may be tempting, but it is important to carefully weigh the ethical, legal, and risk factors before deciding to use these methods

Chapter 5
Case Studies: Examples of AI in Lottery Prediction

There are already a number of examples of organizations using AI to predict lottery numbers. One of the most well-known is LottoGopher, a lottery pool management company that uses machine learning algorithms to analyze historical data and predict which numbers are most likely to be drawn in the future.

Another example is the UK-based company LottoSocial, which uses AI and data analytics to analyze various factors such as weather patterns and social media trends in order to predict lottery numbers.

These case studies demonstrate the potential of AI to improve the lottery experience for players and highlight the importance of developing transparent and accountable AI systems.

However, it is important to note that these AI systems are still in their early stages, and it remains to be seen how effective they will be in the long term. It is also important to remember that no system can guarantee a win in the lottery, and that players should always participate responsibly and within their means.

Chapter 6
Ethical Considerations: The Debate Over Using AI to Play the Lottery

As with any application of AI, there are important ethical considerations to be taken into account when using machine learning algorithms to predict lottery numbers.

One of the main concerns is the potential for AI systems to be biased in their predictions. If the data used to train the algorithms is biased, the resulting predictions may also be biased. This could potentially lead to a situation where certain groups of people are more likely to win the lottery, while others are disadvantaged.

Another ethical consideration is the potential for AI to be used to manipulate the lottery system for financial gain. If certain individuals or organizations have access to advanced AI systems that allow them to consistently predict winning numbers, they may be able to gain an unfair advantage over other players.

It is important that any use of AI in lottery prediction is transparent and accountable, and that steps are taken to ensure that the systems are fair and unbiased. This may include measures such as regular audits and independent testing of the algorithms.

By addressing these ethical considerations, we can ensure that the use of AI in the lottery is a positive development that benefits all players.

Chapter 7
Future of AI in Lottery Prediction: Exploring the Potential and Limitations of AI in Lottery Prediction

In this chapter, we will explore the potential and limitations of using artificial intelligence in lottery prediction. We will start by discussing the current state of AI in lottery prediction, including the types of algorithms and technologies that are being used and the level of success they have achieved. We will then examine the potential future developments in AI, including the role of quantum computing and the potential for even more advanced technologies to be applied to lottery prediction.

Next, we will delve into the limitations of AI in lottery prediction, including the inherent uncertainty of predicting random events and the potential for bias in the data and algorithms. We will also discuss the ethical and legal considerations of using AI in lottery prediction, including the potential for AI to be used to manipulate the odds or for individuals to use AI in an unfair or unethical manner.

Finally, we will explore the potential future of AI in lottery prediction, including the potential for AI to be used in new and innovative ways to improve the accuracy and reliability of predictions. We will also discuss the potential for AI to be used in combination with other technologies and strategies, such as traditional probability analysis and psychological techniques, to further improve the chances of winning. By the end of this chapter, you will have a comprehensive understanding of the potential and limitations of AI in lottery prediction and the role it may play in the future.

The current state of AI in lottery prediction is still in the early stages of development. While there have been some successes in using AI to make more informed predictions, there are also significant limitations to consider. One potential benefit of using AI in lottery prediction is the ability to analyze large amounts of data quickly and identify patterns and trends that may not be immediately apparent to human analysts. This can help to improve the accuracy of predictions and increase the chances of winning.

However, there are also several limitations to consider. One challenge is the quality and quantity of data available for analysis. In order to train effective machine learning models, it is important to have a large and diverse dataset to work with. However, this can be difficult to obtain in the case of lottery prediction, as the number of possible combinations is vast and there is limited historical data available.

Another challenge is the inherent randomness of the lottery. While AI can be effective at identifying patterns and trends, it is still subject to the laws of probability and cannot completely eliminate the element of chance. This means that there is always a certain level of uncertainty when using AI for lottery prediction.

Overall, the potential and limitations of using AI in lottery prediction will depend on the specific application and the resources and data available. As the field of AI continues to advance, it is likely that we will see further developments in this area and a better understanding of the potential and limitations of using AI for lottery prediction.

Conclusion
The Impact of AI on Lottery Prediction and the Future of Gambling

As AI technology continues to advance, it is likely that we will see more and more organizations using machine learning algorithms to predict lottery numbers.

While it is still too early to say how effective these AI systems will be in the long term, they have the potential to revolutionize the way that people play the lottery. By using data-driven predictions, players may be able to increase their chances of winning, and organizations may be able to offer more personalized and engaging lottery experiences.

However, it is important that the use of AI in lottery prediction is approached with caution, and that the ethical considerations discussed in this book are carefully considered. By ensuring that AI systems are transparent, accountable, and fair, we can ensure that the use of AI in the lottery is a positive development for all players.

Ultimately, the future of AI in lottery prediction is an exciting one, full of potential and opportunity. As the technology continues to evolve, we can look forward to a future where the use of AI in the lottery helps to make the experience more enjoyable and rewarding for all players.

Bonus Chapter

In this bonus chapter, we will explore alternative methods for increasing your chances of winning the lottery. While artificial intelligence and machine learning can be powerful tools for predicting lottery numbers, they are not the only options available. In this chapter, we will discuss traditional strategies for selecting lottery numbers, such as using birthdays or lucky numbers, as well as psychological techniques for improving your mindset and increasing your chances of success. We will also discuss the limitations of these methods and the importance of having realistic expectations when it comes to winning the lottery. By the end of this chapter, you will have a well-rounded understanding of the various approaches to increasing your chances of winning the lottery.

There are many traditional strategies that people use to select lottery numbers. Some of the most common strategies include:

1. Birthdays and other personal dates: Many people choose numbers based on their own birthdays or those of their friends and family.
2. Quick picks: Some players opt for a quick pick, where the numbers are selected randomly by the computer.

3. Patterns: Some players believe that certain patterns on the lottery ticket, such as diagonal or horizontal lines, are more likely to be drawn.
4. Lucky numbers: Some people choose numbers that they consider to be lucky, such as 7 or 11.
5. Hot and cold numbers: Some players choose numbers that have been drawn frequently in the past (hot numbers) or those that have not been drawn in a while (cold numbers).
6. Mathematical formulas: Some players use mathematical formulas or algorithms to select their numbers.
7. Personal preferences: Some people choose numbers that have personal meaning to them, such as their favorite sports team or their lucky color.

There are many different mathematical formulas and algorithms that people use to try to improve their chances of winning the lottery. Here are a few examples:

1. Combinatorics: This involves using combinatorial mathematics to analyze the frequency of different number combinations.

2. Probability theory: This involves using probability theory to calculate the likelihood of different number combinations.

3. Statistical analysis: This involves using statistical techniques such as regression analysis to identify patterns and trends in past winning numbers.

4. Random number generation: This involves using algorithms to generate random numbers as a way to increase the diversity of the numbers you play.

5. Hot and cold numbers: This involves selecting numbers that have been drawn more or less frequently in the past, based on the belief that certain numbers are "due" to be drawn.

Example: One example of combinatorics in the context of selecting lottery numbers is the use of combinatorial designs, such as Latin squares or balanced incomplete block designs. These designs allow players to select a small set of numbers that can be combined in different ways to generate a larger set of potential number combinations. For example, a player may choose 5 numbers from a pool of 50, and use a Latin square to generate 25 additional combinations from those 5 numbers. This can increase the player's chances of winning, as they are effectively playing more numbers without having to pay for each individual ticket.

One approach to generating a random odd and even equation from 1 to 50 might be to create a list of the numbers 1 through 50 and then shuffle them randomly.

This could be done using a function like the Fisher-Yates shuffle or a similar algorithm. Once the list has been shuffled, you can then divide it into two groups, one for the odd numbers and one for the even numbers. The resulting equation would be a random assortment of odd and even numbers from 1 to 50.

To use the Fisher-Yates shuffle to generate a random odd and even equation from 1 to 50, we would first create an array with all the numbers from 1 to 50. We would then use the Fisher-Yates shuffle algorithm to shuffle the array randomly. Finally, we would select every other number in the shuffled array (either the odd or even numbers) to create our final equation.

Here's the code:

```
# create an array with all the numbers from 1 to 50
numbers = [1, 2, 3, 4, 5, 6, 7, 8, 9, 10, 11, 12, 13, 14, 15, 16,
17, 18, 19, 20, 21, 22, 23, 24, 25, 26, 27, 28, 29, 30, 31, 32,
33, 34, 35, 36, 37, 38, 39, 40, 41, 42, 43, 44, 45, 46, 47, 48,
49, 50]

# use the Fisher-Yates shuffle to shuffle the array randomly
for i from 0 to 49:
  j = random integer between i and 49 (inclusive)
  swap numbers[i] and numbers[j]

# select every other number in the shuffled array to create
our final equation
equation = []
for i from 0 to 49:
  if i is even:
```

```
equation.append(numbers[i])

# print the final equation
print(equation)
```

When playing a sequence, keep it at 2 numbers, ie, 1-2 35-36., 47-48 and mix with odd and even numbers, either 2 odd and 3 even or vice versa.

It's important to note that while these strategies may be based on mathematical principles, they are not guaranteed to increase your chances of winning. The outcome of a lottery draw is always determined by chance.

Good Luck!